# Karl Malone: The Remarkable Story of One of Basketball's Greatest Power Forwards

## An Unauthorized Biography

## By: Clayton Geoffreys

# Table of Contents

# Foreword

Karl Malone was easily one of the greatest power forwards to ever play the game of basketball. Muscling around the paint over the course of his nineteen-year career in the NBA, Malone was known as a reliable force to be reckoned with. Though he never did win an NBA championship, Malone created a lasting legacy alongside star point-guard John Stockton in the city of Utah. To this day, no player can ever wear the number 32 in Utah as the team lifted Malone's number to the rafters in 2006. Thank you for purchasing *Karl Malone: The Remarkable Story of One of Basketball's Greatest Power Forwards*. In this unauthorized biography, we will learn Karl Malone's incredible life story and impact on the game of basketball. Hope you enjoy and if you do, please do not forget to leave a review!

Also, check out my website at claytongeoffreys.com to join my exclusive list where I let you know about my latest books. To thank you for your purchase, you can go to my site to download a free copy of *33 Life Lessons: Success Principles, Career Advice & Habits of Successful People*. In the book, you'll learn from some of the greatest thought leaders of different industries on what it takes to become successful and how to live a great life.

Cheers,

*Clayton Geoffreys*

*Visit me at www.claytongeoffreys.com*

# Introduction

Fans adorned in navy blue and purple at the Delta Center in Salt Lake City watched as one of their past heroes officially became an immortal when his number was raised to the rafters. There, it would hang forever as a testament to the legend that the man was and will forever be. On March 23, 2006, the Utah Jazz retired the number 32 before they took on the Washington Wizards. The number 32 had become forever synonymous with consistent delivery and the hard work of the player known as "The Mailman" for fans of the Jazz. That man was called that because, when the team needed him, he always delivered. Always. Karl Malone spent the first 18 years of his professional NBA career with the Jazz, forming a historic partnership with his teammate and fellow Hall-of-Famer John Stockton before joining the Los Angeles Lakers for his final year.

Together with teammate John Stockton, Karl Malone was half of the deadliest pick-and-roll combo in the history of the NBA. Stockton was one of the most gifted passers ever to play in the NBA. On the other hand, Karl Malone had a unique combination of size and athleticism that helped him attack the basket off of passes. Put Stockton and Malone together, and you'd have a duo deadlier than most any other in any history. Basketball commentators may have already mentioned the phrase "Stockton to Malone" thousands of times because that's how the duo operated. John found a way to feed Karl, and the latter scored. That's why the Stockton and Malone duo were synonymous with the pick-and-roll.

But The Mailman was not a great player just because of John Stockton. Individually, Malone is considered by many to be one of the greatest power forwards of all time in the NBA. Though that belief has withered over the years, especially with Tim Duncan winning titles for the San Antonio Spurs, Karl Malone still has a legitimate claim to that title. That's saying a lot, considering that the NBA has seen its share of great power forwards like Charles Barkley, Kevin Garnett, Dirk Nowitzki, and many more. Even as younger and more polished power forwards graced the NBA floor, their accomplishments seem to pale in comparison to what The Mailman did throughout his career.

With 36,928 points in his 19 professional seasons, he has the second highest amount of points ever among players. But Karl Malone did not reach that number because he was scoring 40 to 50 points every game. He did that by staying healthy and in shape throughout a career that spanned almost two decades. Even when he was nearing 40 years old, Karl Malone was still playing better than power forwards two decades younger. To add to his accomplishments, The Mailman was chosen MVP of the league twice, was named to the All-NBA team 11 times, and made the All-Star team 14 times. If there is anything more needed to further cement his legacy in basketball, Malone was a part of the historic "Dream Team," representing the United States national team during both the 1992 Barcelona and 1996 Atlanta Summer Olympic games, which resulted in gold medals on both occasions.

At the same time, there are a few critics who argue that Malone is one of basketball's biggest villains. Malone had a body made of muscle. Standing at 6'9", he weighed 256 pounds with less than 5% body fat that he threw around – particularly his elbows. Several instances involving The

Mailman elbowing rival players stirred up controversies during his playing career. Fines and suspensions came Malone's way and sometimes blemished the view that fans had of him. With that kind of size and that penchant for physicality, you may even say that Karl Malone belonged to a pro wrestling ring more than the basketball court.

Nevertheless, Karl Malone has done so much for the game of basketball that you can hardly call him a villain after knowing about his celebrated NBA career. While an NBA championship always eluded him, it does not diminish his status as one of the all-time greats in basketball. The accomplishments of Malone's basketball career are indeed extraordinary, but so too are the circumstances that paved the way for them to be possible.

# Chapter 1: Childhood and Early Life

Karl Malone was born on July 24, 1963, in Summerfield, Louisiana. Born to Shedrick Hay and Shirley Malone, Karl was the youngest boy of nine children. His father left the family when Karl was only 4 years old, leaving the future superstar and his older siblings to be raised in a single parent household. While his father raised a family with another woman, the Malones lived on a farm in Mount Sinai where Karl would work and develop lifelong hobbies such as hunting and fishing, which were born out of necessity for food and not sport.

As a youngster, The Mailman was the furthest thing from a future NBA Hall-of-Famer. He was tremendously skinny and regularly acted out in town as a child. Malone has said that his mother should have given him more "whuppings" during this time so that he could have changed into the man that he is now, sooner. He also never dreamed of being a basketball player the way so many athletes do in their younger years. Instead, as a kid Malone dreamed of owning and driving a tractor trailer rather than shooting hoops each night in front of thousands of screaming people and a nation that all knew his name.

There was no bigger influence in his life than his mother, Shirley. After his father left, Shirley Malone began working three different jobs, including one at a sawmill, to help support her family and give her children a good chance at a future. No matter how bad the family's situation got, Shirley refused welfare or any other kind of assistance. She was determined to stand on her own two feet and show everyone around the family that it was possible for her to succeed no matter how much the odds were stacked against her. As one can see, it's from his mother that Karl Malone picked up his nature of working hard, both mentally and physically. This work ethic would go on to be his biggest character trait throughout his professional career and his life off the court. Shirley would also become his best friend, whom he could take hunting and fishing, as well as being the one person that he could tell anything to—no matter what the topic. Apart from these things, Shirley also instilled strong moral values into Karl. She told him that he needed to forgive his father for abandoning his siblings and himself rather than allowing any anger to take hold of him and make him into a bad person. The effort and values that Shirley Malone labored into her son benefited him greatly, molding him into the man that he would become and distancing him from the young boy who had so frequently got into trouble around town.

# Chapter 2: High School Years

After turning his life around, Karl Malone took an interest in basketball. However, there was not any spare change in his mother's pocket to buy him a hoop so that he could practice his shots, lay-ups, or dunks. As an answer to this problem affecting her son's extracurricular activities, Shirley made a makeshift hoop out of her own arms. She would stand with her arms outstretched, so as to resemble a hoop, and would let Karl practice shooting the ball through her arms instead of allowing him to take up football as his sport of choice because she was concerned about safety and her son's health.

At this time, Malone started to sprout up and change from the scrawny boy that Summerfield and Mount Sinai knew. He grew to become 6'9—towering over many of the other boys his age. His jobs on the farm, as well as roughhousing from his older brothers, toughened him up. His strength came from an unusual job he had, where he wrestled hogs all day to put nose rings on them. He was now beginning to resemble the body structure that he is so well known for having during his professional career—resembling more a bodybuilder like Arnold Schwarzenegger than a basketball player like Wilt Chamberlain.

His training regimen began at this time—disciplining himself to perform running drills, Stairmaster routines, weightlifting intensely, and doing work on the farm, such as bailing hay, in the sweltering heat. Proving he was as mentally tough as physically, Malone refused to work out in air-conditioned gyms. Instead, he preferred the drenching sweat caused by the humidity that other athletes avoid. The conditioning that Malone has always put into his body is what always propelled him to having advantages over his opponents and his teammates.

This advantage is something that Malone worked harder than anyone for, saying "I don't do it for fun, and I don't do it for glory. I do it because it's necessary. I feel my strength and endurance give me an advantage, and I want to keep that advantage."

He began school at Summerfield High School in 1978, a year after his father committed suicide. He made the Rebels' varsity team and became a leader on the court.

Throughout his entire high school career, he averaged 30 points and 20 rebounds a game. His pure basketball skill and physicality paved the way for Summerfield success. From 1979 to 1981, the Summerfield Rebels won three straight Louisiana State Class C championships on the back of the standout player that Malone had become.

Despite tremendous performances on the court, Malone struggled in the classroom. When it came to basketball, he was by far the team's best player. However, his grades proved that he was far from being a standout academically. These poor grades were the biggest problem that Malone suffered throughout his high school career. In fact, they hampered him so badly that he had come extraordinarily close to blowing his chances of playing basketball past high school and into college.

Looking past these less than pleasing grades that Malone was making, the University of Arkansas came calling. Coach Eddie Sutton had taken over for the struggling school in 1974, replacing Lanny Van Eman. He had previously coached college ball at Creighton and the College of Southern Idaho. Sutton had been working on building Arkansas into a formidable foe for the schools that they faced, so naturally he took a great interest in recruiting Malone to be a part of his creation. Sutton's Arkansas team had won the Southwestern Conference regular season championship in 1977, 1978, and 1979. He had also achieved the Southwestern Conference tournament championship in 1977 and 1979 and, though he did not win that title in 1978, his team did reach the Final Four that year.

Despite the fact that Karl desired to join Sutton and play for Arkansas, his mother had other plans. She knew the grades that her son was making in high school were not good enough and urged him to attend Louisiana Tech instead. Louisiana Tech basketball coach Andy Russo had been struggling to recruit players, losing many to rival schools right from out under his nose. Suddenly, he received a phone call from Shirley Malone. Shirley told Russo that Karl was coming to play for Louisiana Tech, though Russo knew that Karl was heavily interested in joining Eddie Sutton's Arkansas team.

The Louisiana Tech Bulldogs had managed only six seasons where they reached 20 wins in their entire school history. How was a team so well known for losing going to compete for attention with the big boys of Arkansas?

"We would always read in the paper that he's going to Arkansas and we knew Karl wanted to go to Arkansas so we would call her back and say `Are you sure he's coming to Louisiana Tech?' She assured us that he was coming," Russo said, speaking to the Bulldogs' website 28 years after Malone's college career ended.

It was the constant urging and motherly tenacity that caused Malone to eventually meet up with Russo in Summerfield and sign the necessary paperwork to become a Bulldog. Russo swept in right before Sutton and his boys from Arkansas could, as they were on their way for Malone to put pen to paper and join their team.

"There was no question in my mind that he came to Louisiana Tech because his mother made him come here," Russo said, reflecting on that moment where he had finally snagged a top recruit. "If anybody says any different, they are lying."

The 6'9, 230-pound Karl Malone found himself going to Ruston in August, when fall semester started at Louisiana Tech.

# Chapter 3: College Years at Louisiana Tech

As previously stated, if anything ever got in the way of the freight train that was Karl Malone, it was academics. His grades continued to suffer during his freshman year at Louisiana Tech and he was ruled academically ineligible to play for the basketball team until his grades improved. Being unable to play the sport he loved because of an old obstacle really got to Malone, who applied his bedrock work ethic to better his academic marks. He was not the only person he did not want to let down, though. Karl remembered how his mother always wanted him to work harder than anyone else and be great. Going to college may have been an achievement for a boy from a family who struggled to get by, but it was not going to be worth a grain of salt if he struggled and failed out. Instead, he began to carry his books the way he once did hay and he wrestled with his homework as if they were the hogs he once tried to put nose rings on. His freshman year of hard work reaped the ultimate rewards, as he was able to play for the Bulldogs in his sophomore year.

Coach Russo had built a supporting cast of players through recruitments that would benefit both Karl and the Louisiana Bulldogs team. When Malone was finally eligible, Russo noted that he had tremendous strength and lightning-quick speed despite his muscular build.

"He was the fastest and the strongest guy we had," Russo said. "During the first practice he broke a backboard and when we worked out, he broke a machine in the weight room."

Indeed, the sheer power that Malone had worked on throughout his teenage years was a huge aid now, but it tended to rack up quite the expense when it came to equipment. Things such as backboards and gym machines just were not able to handle the might that he possessed throughout his body. In time, opposing teams were absolutely unable to deal with it, either.

In his first season with the team, the Bulldogs played 27 games. They finished the season with a record of 18-9, two wins shy of reaching 20 wins for only the seventh time in school history. They were bounced out of the Southland

Conference Tournament early on by North Texas, losing 87-73. This loss was in spite of a decent record in the Southland Conference, where they had only lost 4 games out of 13. Karl Malone led the team in every statistic by a stretch. He was averaging 20.9 points whereas Willie Simons, his closest competition on the team, was averaging only 9.6.

His second year with the team is when things really got going. After Malone broke his second backboard, the Bulldogs' sports information director, Keith Prince, sent pieces of the shattered glass to major sports periodicals. *Sports Illustrated* even ran an article about the situation, spreading it across the nation to readers and sports fans everywhere. This attracted a lot of attention to Malone, but where the true attention came from was his performances on the court and the number of points he was racking up. Due to the consistent and reliable style of his performances, a local sportswriter nicknamed Malone "The Mailman." Averaging 18.7 points, Malone led the Bulldogs to a 26-7 season that earned Louisiana Tech the Southland Conference Tournament Title. By winning this title, the

Bulldogs gained a place in the NCAA tournament—a first in school history.

And so it was in the first round of this prestigious tournament that the hype surrounding "The Mailman" only escalated further. Facing off against Fresno State, he threw down a one-handed alley-oop dunk that caused jaws to drop and ESPN to show a highlight clip of the moment again and again—he was a national sensation.

Despite bowing to Houston in the next game, the following year for Malone was his biggest yet. The people and the press remembered what he had achieved the year before and saw him as the next big thing. "His last year was the most sustained amount of media coverage over a period that I had in my 25 years here," Keith Prince said. "That whole season we were dealing with the national press."

An extraordinary 10-0 start to the season saw Louisiana Tech break into the Top 25 and eventually the Top 10 in the nation. The season would end a school best 29-3 for the Bulldogs, who rewarded themselves with a conference title and a place in the NCAA Sweet Sixteen for their troubles.

After defeating Pittsburgh and Ohio State, Tech fell 86-84 to Oklahoma in overtime. Malone averaged 16.5 points in his final season with the Bulldogs. After capturing three All-American team awards, he was ready to declare for the 1985 NBA Draft.

# Chapter 4: Karl's NBA Career

## Getting Drafted

Coming into the NBA Draft, Karl Malone was a legitimate 6'9" power forward. His height was about average for a player at that position; the astonishing thing about him was that he already had what people call an "NBA body." That means that his build was mature enough to play in the NBA. But actually, Malone's size was already way beyond what was needed to be in the NBA. He came into the draft a lot more muscular and cut than the typical young NBA prospect. Even at the NBA level, his physique was good enough to dominate and bang with veteran big men. Not only was he built rock-hard and solid, but he was much better conditioned and more athletic than any other power forward out there. Karl was a freak of nature in the positive sense of the phrase.

While Karl Malone was a physical specimen in his own right, he also had skills as a power forward. He earned the nickname "The Mailman" back in college because he knew how to deliver whenever the team needed him to. He had offensive gifts even then. Malone shot an average of 56.6% during his three-year stay with Louisiana Tech. That meant that Karl was a strong finisher at the power forward spot. Aside from finishing, he also showed a few flashes of his perimeter games even back in college. And, overall, he was a pretty good rebounder.

Pro scouts, however, did not see Malone the way the rest of the nation did. They were impressed by his unique build and hard work, but they preferred to look at the fact that, during his time with the Bulldogs, his numbers got worse each season. The scouts also were not convinced by him because of his failure to make the 1984 USA Olympic basketball team, which at that time was still using college and amateur players and would continue to do so until the 1992 games.

Due to what these scouts were saying about him, his value to NBA teams dropped. When it came time for the draft, Patrick Ewing from Georgetown was picked first, then Wayman Tisdale from the Oklahoma team that eliminated Malone's Bulldogs. Tisdale was believed to be the best power forward in the crop. Back in college, he scored, rebounded, and blocked shots better than what Malone did. People believed Malone was the inferior player, and they had reasons to believe that. Time and time again, Karl saw others picked before him when he previously believed he wouldn't have to wait so long.

Despite the way the draft was turning out, Malone had a strong gut feeling that he could not ignore. He fully believed that the Dallas Mavericks would make him their first selection with the eighth pick in the first round. In fact, he was so sure that he had already made his way down to Dallas and purchased an apartment to live in until he could buy permanent housing with the money he would be making. However, the Mavericks opted to go for Detlef Schrempf of West Germany, who had played college ball for the University of Washington. Four more picks passed by and still nobody selected "The Mailman," until, with the 13th pick, the Utah Jazz came in to snag him.

The Jazz had long had an eye on Karl Malone even before the NBA Draft. They were contemplating him as a one of the guys they would take with their pick. They were impressed at how The Mailman could deliver and rebound at a pretty good rate. They also had their eye on a power forward named Keith Lee. Thinking that Malone would end up with the teams that had higher draft picks, Lee was their man.

But they were surprised on draft day. Malone was slipping down. None of the other teams was interested in him. Frank Layden, the Utah coach who was also the team's general manager, was surprised. He even worried because he wondered why The Mailman was so unattractive to the other teams. At first, he thought there was something wrong with Karl Malone from a physical standpoint.[i] But that was not the case. Karl was a fitness freak. He never had any serious physical ailments.

Meanwhile, Layden, before drafting Malone, was getting different versions of why the Louisiana Tech power forward was not getting the attention he deserved. Al Bianchi, an assistant with the Phoenix Suns, said he did not bother with Karl Malone because he thought he was "too nice." On the other hand, another story was the complete opposite. Layden had found out that Malone was not even favored by his college coach. Rumors came out that he was uncoachable and that his temper was tough to handle. However, Layden gave Karl a chance, especially because Keith Lee, their other option, had already been taken two picks earlier. If he didn't, he would have passed out on the biggest steal of the 1985 NBA Draft.[ii]

The Jazz had been struggling in recent years, losing money despite efforts to make a profit by staging events such as playing games in Las Vegas. The team played in the smallest market in the NBA, which offered no support when the team selected an unknown player named John Stockton in the draft the year prior. By grabbing Malone, the Jazz and Layden hoped to turn the team's fortunes around and start bringing fans into the stands. Karl's apartment in Dallas would have to be sold, of course, for Salt Lake City was quite another world away. When Layden went on to announce their pick, he told the Jazz faithful that they were "going to bring a Mailman to Utah." When Stockton was drafted exactly a year before, the Jazz crowd booed him. But, when Layden announced Malone's arrival, the crowd collectively gave their approval by cheering hard.[iii]

## Rookie Season

Karl worked hard to disprove what the pro scouts had seen when they reported back to their teams before the draft. He was also on a mission to show the 12 teams that passed on him that they were wrong to select other players instead of him. At the young age of 22, the rookie Malone started 76 out of 81 regular season games for the Jazz while John Stockton, the big draft pick from the previous year, was mostly a sixth man coming off of the bench.

Malone added much-needed assistance for the Jazz's star player, Adrian Dantley. He was the Jazz's second-best scorer and best rebounder. However, his rookie season did not start as well as people might have hoped for. He did not get a lot of minutes in his first few games. Though Malone had two double-double performances in his first five games, his scoring was not as good as it might have been. He played only about 23 minutes per game and his scoring high was 14 points.

Early in the season, Karl Malone was more of a rebounder than a scorer. He had a few double-double performances in the first 20 games of the season, but his scoring was still subpar at best. But then he had a breakout performance in an overtime loss to the Los Angeles Lakers on December 4, 1985. He scored 25 points and grabbed 15 rebounds in 44 minutes of play. He shot 11 out of 16 from the field in that game. Karl Malone would not look back after that.

Malone had three straight 20-point games in December. All three games were victories. Two of those games were also double-double performances. In the third one, he even had 5 steals to go along with his 25 points. On January 14, 1986, he scored his season high of 29 points in a win against the Houston Rockets. He also had 14 rebounds in that outing. His rebounding high that season was 15, which he reached on three different occasions.

Throughout the course of the season, Malone averaged 14.9 points and 8.9 rebounds per game. He had an immediate impact on the Utah Jazz, who had struggled the year before and were eliminated in the second round of the playoffs by the Denver Nuggets. Because of his steady performance as a rookie, he began to prove all of his doubters wrong. He was voted to the All-Rookie team that season. With that, he edged out four other power forwards chosen before him. Karl Malone turned out to be the steal of the 1985 NBA Draft. As good as he was, Karl was not the Rookie of the Year that season because Patrick Ewing's All-Star rookie season was just too tough to top. Despite that, Malone was still able to help his team win 42 out of 82 games that season.

The Jazz returned to the playoffs again during this rookie season, making it three consecutive times that they had accomplished this. However, they did not get to enjoy the moment long. The Dallas Mavericks, who had passed on Malone during the draft, eliminated the Jazz in four games. Those four games displayed an improvement in Malone's scoring, which increased from 14.9 to 20 points a game. He continued to struggle at the free throw line, however, and was underwhelming when it came to rebounding. As seen in previous times of his life though, when Malone struggled he found a way to improve himself and only grow stronger.

## Improvement Season, Utah's Go-to Guy

The performance of Malone during his rookie season, which had seen him named to All-Rookie team and finishing third in Rookie of the Year voting, caused the Jazz to undergo change before the 1986-1987 season. Star player Adrian Dantley was traded to Detroit for Kelly Tripucka, who spent most of his time on the bench. This showed that the Jazz was making way for Malone to be the star of their team. Despite Dantley averaging nearly 30 points per game in the previous season, the Utah Jazz front office believed that their future lay on the broad shoulders of Karl Malone. Many other players from the bench would be inserted into the starting lineups during the year whether because of injuries or as a changing of the guard.

Malone did not disappoint the Jazz in his second season. He was already the go-to guy on offense. In the second game of the 1986-87 season, Karl scored 24 points and a new career-high 17 rebounds. In just his first 20 games, Malone had already piled up 10 double-doubles. He had five straight double-double games in scoring and rebounding. Four of those five games were 20-10 scoring-rebounding games. That's how much improvement Karl was showing early in the season. The Mailman did indeed know how to deliver.

On January 13, 1987, Karl Malone scored a new career-high 38 points against the Portland Trailblazers. In that loss, he also had 16 rebounds and 6 assists. As steady and as good as Malone was playing that season, he was not chosen as an All-Star. Nevertheless, The Mailman continued to deliver great performances. He broke the 30-point barrier yet again as he scored 36 in a loss against the Washington Bullets. He had 15 rebounds that night. In a blowout win over the Seattle SuperSonics, Malone scored 38 again while also grabbing 13 rebounds. He was even better as the season was winding down. From March until April, Malone scored more than 30 points six times. Two of those were back-to-back performances while four were double-doubles.

By the end of the season, unpopular point guard John Stockton was beginning to start games and get more playing time. Malone was averaging 21.9 points and 10.4 rebounds while shooting 51.2% from the floor that season, which saw the 44-38 Jazz make the playoffs again. Karl Malone had 52 double-double games that season while playing all 82 games for the Jazz.

Coming into the playoffs, they were the fourth seed in the West. However, they lost to the Golden State Warriors in five games in the first round. Malone was anything but disappointing in that series as he averaged 20 points and 9.6 rebounds in five games. However, it was obvious that he was struggling against the Warrior defense, as he merely shot 42% from the floor. Though the Jazz had won the first two games, the Warriors found a way to win the next three to eliminate Utah from contention. Though it was a disappointing end to the season, Karl Malone was a bright spot for the team as he showed marked improvements to his game as the Jazz's best player.

## First All-Star Season

In the 1987-88 seasons, things turned around for the Jazz. Karl Malone was now the official offensive superstar of the team and John Stockton was now the starting point guard who was showing that he was the commanding general of the court. It was in that season that the Stockton-Malone combo reached its fruition. Karl Malone had all the offensive weapons needed by a dominant power forward. Meanwhile, Stockton's passing abilities were second to none. It was a match made in heaven as Stockton would constantly find and feed his big man for easy baskets. Malone, as his nickname suggested, always delivered for his point guard.

Malone came out smoking in the new season. He scored more than 20 points in each of his first nine games. Three of those were 30-point games and five were double-double performances. In just his first 20 games, Karl Malone already had 12 double-doubles and five 30-point outings. As good as he already had been in his second season, Malone was shaping up to be even better in his third year as a professional basketball player.

On January 20, 1988, Karl Malone established a new career high of 39 points in a loss to the Detroit Pistons. He also had 13 rebounds in that game, which was the third of five straight double-double outings. He had the game of his life in a high-scoring 3-point win over the Portland Trailblazers on February 4. Karl scored a new career high of 41 points while also grabbing a new high of 19 rebounds. He dished out 7 assists in that game. That performance was the fifth one of a five-game double-double streak.

Because of Karl Malone's performances that season, he was selected to his first All-Star Game appearance. After All-Star break, he immediately went back to work. From February 20 to March 12, Malone had an amazing 11-game stretch. He scored 32 on February 20 in a win against the Clippers. He then had 38 points and 17 rebounds four nights later versus the Denver Nuggets. Two nights later, Karl Malone scored 41 again in a win against the Sacramento Kings. He had 15 rebounds that night. On March 5, he put up 38 points, 13 rebounds, and 7 assists versus the San Antonio Spurs. After that game, he had back-to-back big rebounding games, with 19 against the New Jersey Nets and then 18 against Detroit. In that 11-game stretch, Karl Malone averaged 31.7 points and 14.3 rebounds. He had nine double-doubles and six games of scoring more than 30 over that span.

If you think that performance was incredible, Karl Malone would replicate, if not outdo, those feats. From April 11 to the 23rd, Malone had double-double performances in all eight of Utah's final games. He even recorded 33 points and 20 rebounds in a win against the LA Clippers on April

20. Two nights later, he scored 41 points and grabbed 18 rebounds against the SuperSonics. He averaged 36.9 points and 14.9 rebounds in that eight-game stretch. He was simply amazing to watch that season.

With averages of 27.7 points and 12 rebounds per game, Malone established himself as one of the most dominant power forwards in the league. Aided also by Stockton's 14.7 points and 13.8 assists per game, the Jazz finished the season 47-35 as they marched into the playoffs as the fifth seed in the Western Conference. Malone ended the season strong. One can only surmise that he would continue playing the same way in the playoffs.

The Jazz breezed past the Portland Trail Blazers in the first round of the playoffs, winning three games out of four to advance to the next round. After scoring only 16 in the opening game loss of that series, Malone carried his team to three straight wins by scoring 37, 35, and 38. The Blazers had no answer for Malone as he almost singlehandedly destroyed the Portland-based team.

In the next round, they found themselves up against the historical powerhouse of the Los Angeles Lakers, who just happened to be the defending champions. The Lakers took the first game of the series at the Staples Center, but Games 2 and 3 went to the Jazz. Malone scored 29 in each of those games. The Lakers recovered, winning both Games 4 and 5. Karl had 29 and 27 in those two losses. The Jazz refused to go away, though, and their persistence was rewarded with a big 108-80 win in Game 6—tying the series at three games apiece. The Mailman delivered 27 points.

Though the Lakers ended up winning the series, the Jazz had shown the basketball world that they would no longer allow themselves to be pushed around as they had been during their early years in Salt Lake City. Malone especially showed that he was a superstar, putting up 31 points in the seventh game. Even as the Jazz lost that series, Karl Malone averaged 29 points and 10.1 rebounds in seven games. He was already a legitimate superstar in just his third season as an NBA player.

## First-Round Exits

During the offseason, Karl Malone was awarded for his performances with a 10-year contract worth $18 million per year. During the 1988-89 season, Frank Layden resigned as coach and was promoted to team president, paving the way for the now legendary Jerry Sloan to take over as coach. Under Sloan's direction, the partnership of Malone and Stockton proved to be dynamic. Their pick-and-roll combo had reached a level unseen in the history of the NBA.

With Stockton feeding him for easy baskets, Karl Malone reached new heights in his offensive game. Merely at the start of the season, Malone was already scoring in bunches. He opened the 1988-89 season scoring 36 and 35 in his first two games. In just his fourth game of the season, The Mailman delivered a career-high 22 rebounds for the Jazz to go along with 35 points. Just three nights later, he scored 36 points against the Pacers in the middle of November.

On November 19, 1988, Malone exploded for 42 points on 14 of 19 shooting. While free throw shooting was always one of his weaknesses, he was 14 of 14 in that game. At that point in his career, Karl's free throw woes were slowly disappearing. Malone led the Utah Jazz to an 8-2 record in the early part of the season. In their first 10 games, the Jazz even had a seven-game winning streak. Through the first 20 games, Karl Malone scored less than 20 points only twice.

On December 17, Karl Malone recorded a new career high in points. He scored 44 on 15 of 22 shooting from the floor while also grabbing 13 boards. However, that effort came in a loss. That performance was in a stretch of six straight games in which Malone scored more than 30 points. For the second straight season, Karl Malone was selected to take part in the All-Star Game together with Stockton, who was selected for his first appearance. Malone scored 29 points in the midseason classic and was named the All-Star MVP.

Malone finished second in scoring only to Michael Jordan, averaging 29.1 points and 10.7 rebounds. Under Sloan, Malone was slowly improving his playmaking, as his assists increased to almost 3 per game. He was so good and dominant that season that he finished third in the MVP voting behind only Magic Johnson and Michael Jordan. Nevertheless, he was named to his first All-NBA First Team selection.

Despite a 51-31 season and a second seed in the Western Conference in Sloan's first year of tenure, the Jazz were swept away in the first round of the playoffs by the Warriors. For some reason, they could not beat the seventh-seeded Warriors team. Malone had a pedestrian 22-point game in Game 1. Though he exploded for 37 and 33 in the next two games, the Jazz just could not get over the run-and-gun Golden State team.

For the 1989-90 season, the Utah Jazz retained their core players. The team was still running on the combo of Stockton and Malone. Stockton was still delivering passes to Malone while The Mailman delivered at a high rate. At 26 years old, Malone was entering the prime of his playing career. It was only his fifth season, but it seemed as if he'd been in the NBA for more than that because of how he dominated the league.

In the Utah Jazz's season opener, Karl Malone immediately went back to work scoring 40 points and grabbing 16 rebounds. In his first 20 games, he never scored less than 20 points. From being merely a 13th pick five years before, The Mailman was now delivering great games night in and night out.

Against the Charlotte Hornets on December 22, 1989, Karl Malone delivered his first 50-point game. He erupted for 52 points on 22 of 28 shooting from the field. He also had 17 rebounds in that career night. He did not slow down, as he scored 48 two weeks later in a game against the Denver Nuggets on January 6, 1990.

Just when you thought Karl Malone would not outdo his 52-point game, he wowed everyone with his new career performance against the Milwaukee Bucks on January 27. He scored 61 points while grabbing 18 rebounds. He shot 21 of 26 from the field and 19 of 23 from the foul line. Though that was not a franchise record, it was the most points a player had put up ever since the Jazz relocated from New Orleans to Utah. What was amazing about that performance was that Malone only had to play 33 minutes because the game ended up as a 48-point blowout. Had he played an extra 10 more minutes, he could have scored at least 70 points. But Karl Malone cared more about winning than setting records.

After that amazing performance, Malone scored 40 or more in five more outings. For the third straight season, he was an All-Star. But Malone had to miss that game because of an ankle injury. However, he still played all 82 games of the season while averaging 31 points, 11 rebounds, 2.8 assists, and 1.5 steals. He shot a career-high 56.2% from the floor. For the second straight season, Karl Malone was named to the All-NBA First Team and was bridesmaid to Michael Jordan in the scoring championship race. He finished fourth in MVP voting, as he led the Utah Jazz to the fourth seed in the West with a record of 55-27.

Despite a good seeding, the Utah Jazz once again fell in the first round. For some reason, Karl Malone struggled against the defense of the Phoenix Suns. After winning Game 1 by 17 points, Malone and company lost the next two games. Malone was a 30-point scorer in the regular season, but his scoring fell to the low 20s in his first three playoff games that season. He broke out with 33 points in Game 4, helping his team to force a deciding Game 5. However, he still could not get over the Suns defense and he was limited to 26 in the deciding game that went the way of the Suns in a tight contest. After scoring 31 points per game in the regular season, Malone was limited to an average of 25.2 points in that five-game series against the Suns and Utah was once again headed home early in the playoffs.

## Breaking Out of the First Round, Second-Round Exit

Prior to the 1990-91 season, the Utah Jazz bolstered their starting lineup by adding former All-Star and veteran Jeff Malone, who is not related to Karl Malone. Jeff was an additional scoring threat for the Jazz and was vital in taking some pressure off Karl. Before Jeff Malone's arrival, the Jazz were relying heavily on Karl Malone and Stockton for scoring. An additional scoring option was needed for the Jazz to get to the next level.

Malone started the season strong, as he always did. He scored 30 or more points on three separate occasions in the first 10 games. He even recorded six straight double-doubles from the first game of the regular season of 1990-91. As good as he was, the Jazz initially struggled, going 8-7 in their first 15 games. Nevertheless, the team got their act together and won six straight games. In three of those six games, Karl Malone scored more than 30 points.

From the end of December up to January, The Mailman delivered 13 straight double-double performances. He had 40 points in one of those games and 18 rebounds each in the last two outings. In that stretch, the Utah Jazz lost only three times, meaning that the team was nearly unbeatable whenever Karl Malone was delivering great performances. For the fourth straight season, Malone was an All-Star.

He did not slow down even after being named an All-Star for the fourth time. He was the team's best player, and they needed him to perform at his best each and every game. On March 27, 1991, Malone scored his season high of 41 points in a loss to the Los Angeles Clippers. He then scored the same number of points in an 11-point win against the Denver Nuggets just a few games before the end of the regular season.

In his sixth season in the NBA, Karl Malone averaged 29 points, 11.8 rebounds, 3.3 assists, 1.1 steals, and 1 block. While Karl did not have the explosive scoring games that he did the previous season, he did make up for it with his consistency. In the 82 games he played that season, he scored more than 30 points in half of them. In three of those games, he scored 40 or more. With that, he was named to the All-NBA First Team for the third straight year. He led the Jazz to the fifth seed in the West with a 54-28 finish in the regular season.

Karl Malone and the Utah Jazz got their revenge against the Phoenix Suns in the first round of the playoffs. That time, Malone was no longer struggling against the Suns' defense. He recorded 27 points and 10 rebounds in a 39-point beating in Game 1. Though they did give one game away, he had 22 points and 14 boards in Game 2 before scoring 32 and 38 in Games 3 and 4. Both of the final two games were wins for the Jazz.

In the second round, they met the top-seeded Portland Trailblazers, led by Clyde Drexler and Terry Porter. In that series, the Blazers showed why they were the best team in the West. The Jazz were destroyed in Game 1 by 20 points. In that game, Malone was limited to 21 points, though he did have 16 boards. Karl bounced back with a 40-point outing in Game 2 as he led the Jazz to a close win over Portland. However, the Trailblazers still escaped by 2 slim points. Thanks to Malone's 31 points and 21 rebounds in Game 3, Utah was able to get a win, but the Blazers finished the Jazz in the next couple of games to end another playoff run for Utah.

## Breaking Through to the Conference Finals

The 1991-1992 season was the breakthrough year for the Jazz and for Malone as well. They did it by bolstering the defense of the team through the addition of defensive wingman Tyrone Corbin. In exchange for Corbin, they had to give up longtime Jazz player Thurl Bailey. Bailey had been drafted by the team in 1983, was with Utah up until that trade in 1991. The trade helped the Jazz's defense improve. That allowed Stockton, Karl, and Jeff to focus on carrying the team with their offense.

Malone opened the season scoring back-to-back 30-point games. He had 35 and 13 boards in a win against the Minnesota Timberwolves, and then 37 and 13 in a loss against the Indiana Pacers. Malone then had six straight double-double performances near the end of November 1991. Though Utah started the season 1-3, they managed to pull themselves together to win 12 of their first 20 games.

It was that season when the first negative mark was made on Malone's record. On December 14, 1991, he threw a flagrant elbow to the head of Detroit Pistons point guard Isiah Thomas. Thomas needed 40 stitches and Malone was suspended one game as well as fined $10,000 because of that incident. This was the first time that Malone was viewed negatively by fans and sportscasters alike, as some began to see The Mailman as a villain rather than the superstar he was showing himself to be.

From the middle of January 1992 up to February 1992, Karl Malone went on a one-month tear of 16 double-

double performances. The notable ones were his 43 points and 16 rebounds in a tight win against Phoenix, and his 34 points and 21 boards in a close game against the Chicago Bulls. In that amazing stretch of games for The Mailman, the Utah Jazz won 12 out of 16 outings. For the fifth consecutive season, Karl Malone was an All-Star.

He had his best scoring game in a blowout win over the Golden State Warriors on March 3, 1992. He scored 44 points in that game to go along with 11 rebounds and 5 assists. Just over a week later, he scored 40 against the Sacramento Kings in another blowout win. He scored 40 or more points in a game five times over the course of the season as he averaged 28 points, 11.2 rebounds, and 3.2 assists. He was second in scoring yet again to Michael Jordan while being named to the All-NBA First Team for the fourth straight time. He led Utah to the second seed in the West with a record of 55 wins and 27 losses.

In the first round of the playoffs, the Malone and the Jazz absolutely destroyed the Los Angeles Clippers in the first two games. Karl had 32 points and 10 rebounds in an 18-point victory in Game 1. He then delivered 32 points and

13 boards in an 11-point win in Game 2. Though The Mailman and his team were slowed down in a loss in Game 3, Malone went on to score 44 in Game 4. However, the Clippers were still able to tie the series with a win in that game. While Malone was limited to 19 points in Game 5, his team got the better of the Clippers on their way to the second round.

The Jazz squared off against the Seattle SuperSonics in the second round. Malone delivered 28 and 30 in Games 1 and 2 as Utah took both games. They lost Game 3, however. Not wanting to repeat what had happened with the Clippers in the first round, the Jazz closed the series out by winning Games 4 and 5. Karl had 22 and 37 in the final two games of the series. With that easy series win over the Sonics, the Utah Jazz were on their way to their first Western Conference finals appearance.

They lost to the Trail Blazers, but the series demonstrated how strong the Utah team from Utah was. Portland took Games 1 and 2 in blowout fashion. It seemed as if the Jazz did not know what hit them. Malone was not at his best in those games. He had 11 points in Game 1 and then 25 in

Game 2. But the Jazz and their leader showed grit in the next two games. Malone exploded for 39 points in Game 3 to help his team inch one game closer. The Jazz tied the series in Game 4 due in large part to the 33 points and 12 rebounds of The Mailman. Despite valiant efforts by Malone, who had 38 in Game 5 and 19 rebounds in Game 6, the top-seeded Portland team edged them out in six games.

## Another First-Round Loss

In the summer of 1992, Malone was named to the United States basketball team that would travel to Barcelona for the Olympic Games. Malone had been cut from the team eight years before but now that the team was accepting professionals and now that he was showcasing his world-class talent, he was a shoo-in. He put up 13 points alongside players like Magic Johnson, Larry Bird, Michael Jordan, and Jazz teammate John Stockton. The "Dream Team" dominated each of the six teams that they faced and won the gold medal with ease.

After such great recent success for the Jazz, the 1992-93 season proved to be a disappointment. For some reason, the

Utah Jazz just could not replicate their previous successful seasons. Not a lot of changes were implemented to the team. The core remained the same. Some thought that the defense struggled because their center Mark Eaton was already deep into his 30s. Nevertheless, Karl Malone remained a beast.

Malone scored 30 or more points in nine of his first 20 outings. He had 13 double-doubles in those games. He then had six straight double-double outings late in January 1993. After the streak ended, Malone had seven more consecutive double-double performances. In one of those games, Malone surpassed the 16,000-point mark for his career.

Karl Malone was named an All-Star that season as Utah hosted the game. In that midseason classic, he and John Stockton shared All-Star MVP honors, basically playing the way they did as teammates in Utah. Malone scored 28 points and grabbed 10 rebounds while his buddy had 15 dimes, most of which were delivered to The Mailman.

For the season, Karl Malone averaged 27 points, 11.2 rebounds, 3.8 assists, and 1.5 steals. He was named to the All-NBA First Team again, as he was becoming arguably the second-best player (behind Jordan) of that era of NBA basketball. Though it could be considered good for most teams, the Jazz saw their 47-35 record as a step backward. The team was merely the sixth seed in the tough Western Conference. They were eliminated by the Seattle SuperSonics in the first round of the playoffs after finishing third in their division. Malone struggled in that series, averaging 24 points and 10.4 rebounds while shooting 45.4% from the floor. Naturally, Malone and the Jazz were determined to make up for a season remembered only for hosting All-Star weekend.

## Back to the Western Conference Finals

1994 yielded great results for Karl Malone as he entered his ninth year in the NBA. While the team retained their core, they were able to get younger at the center spot by adding Felton Spencer to replace the retired Mark Eaton, who ended his playing years with a career average of 3.5 blocks. That record still stands day as the highest average for shots blocked in an entire career. The team also acquired veteran former All-Star big man Tom Chambers, who used to give Malone fits when he was playing in Phoenix. In the middle of the season, they traded Jeff Malone for shooter Jeff Hornacek.

With more weapons to go to, Karl Malone did not have to score as much as he used to. He was still an offensive powerhouse, however. Malone started the season with eight straight double-double performances. He scored 30 or more points in three of those outings and he grabbed 20 boards in one of them.

Karl Malone did not have a lot of explosive games that season, but he made up for it with his scoring consistency. If he did not erupt for 40 or 50 points in one night, he was scoring 30 or more points in most of his games. Despite a slight dip in scoring, Karl Malone was still a rebounding demon. He rarely had games in which he did not reach double digits in rebounding. For the seventh consecutive year, he was an All-Star.

In a game against the Warriors in March of 1994, Malone had a career-high 23 boards. However, he missed a tremendous number of shots, which cost the Jazz the game. Ever the perfectionist, Malone stated in a post-match interview that his rebounds would not be the highlight the next morning because all anyone would talk about was his missed shots.

He averaged 25.2 points and 11.5 rebounds that season. Though his scoring saw a dip, Malone was still a steady force in the paint because of his terrific rebounding. In all but 22 of his 82 games, he had double digits in rebounding. The Mailman delivered 60 double-double performances in the regular season. Other than that, the other aspects of his game also improved. Malone had a career-high 4 assists per game while also tallying 1.5 steals and blocks. He was never known as a shot blocker, but he put a little more focus on that aspect of his game in that season. The Jazz were back to a 50-win season with a 53-29 record, which was good enough for the fifth seed in the Western Conference.

Despite a 36-point game by Malone in the opener against the Seattle SuperSonics in the first round, the Utah Jazz lost to their foes. They bounced back in the next three games. Though Karl was limited to 7 out of 25 from the field in Game 2, the Jazz won that one by 12 points. Game 3 was a one-sided bout in favor of the Jazz, who won by 33 points. While the Sonics fought tooth and nail to extend the series in Game 4, Malone's 34 points and 12 rebounds were insurmountable.

In the next round, the Utah Jazz banked on their superstar once again to take three straight games from the Denver Nuggets. Karl Malone had 25 points and 10 rebounds in Game 1. He then scored 32 in Game 2. For Game 3, Karl had 26 points, 13 rebounds, and 6 assists. Malone was in a seven-game double-double streak in the playoffs. The Jazz were up 3-0, which is an insurmountable lead in a seven-game playoff series.

However, the Utah Jazz almost made history in a bad way as they lost three straight games to the Nuggets. Malone had poor shooting performances in Games 4 and 5 and Denver escaped with wins. Then, in Game 6, the Jazz had one more chance to dispose of their pesky opponents. However, despite a 31-point, 15-rebound output by Malone, the Nuggets were able to force Game 7. But it seemed like Denver lost gas as the Utah Jazz took Game 7 away from the gritty Nuggets team. Karl Malone had 31 points, 14 rebounds, and 6 assists for the Jazz, who avoided squandering away their 3-0 series lead.

By beating the Denver Nuggets, the Utah Jazz found themselves in the Western Conference finals for only the second time in franchise history. In their way to an NBA finals appearance were the Houston Rockets, led by Hakeem Olajuwon, that season's MVP. Since Michael Jordan had decided to retire before the 1993-94 season, many thought that the NBA title was a sure win for the Western Conference team that got to the finals. If there was a time for Malone to grab his first championship, that was the time to do so, especially with Jordan out of the picture in the East.

However, the top-seeded Rockets won both of their first home-court games. They won Game 1 by 12 and then beat the Jazz in Game 2 by 5 points. In Game 1, Malone could only score 20. Though he had 32 points in Game 2, he could not match Olajuwon's 41 points. Malone scored only 22 points in Game 3, but his team won by 9 points, thanks to the defense they played against the Rockets' main players. That was their lone win in the series. Houston won Game 4 by merely 2 points in a tough, defense-oriented battle. Despite 31 from The Mailman in Game 5, the Rockets still won the game by double figures. With that, the Jazz once again fell short of their first NBA finals.

## New Franchise Win-Loss Record, First-Round Exit

In the 1994-95 season, the Utah team was stronger than ever. It was not just because their duo of Stockton and Malone were playing improved basketball. Their role players were stepping up. Hornacek was an outside threat while guys off the bench like Antoine Carr, Adam Keefe, and Tom Chambers were contributing good second-unit numbers for Utah. The team was slowly coming into its own as the Jazz moved away from relying heavily on their two stars, who were already past 30 years old by then.

Though Malone was slowly moving past his prime playing years at the age of 31 years old, he was still more than capable of putting up amazing numbers every game. In his first 20 outings, The Mailman had 12 double-double performances, and he scored more than 30 points in four of those games. On January 16, 1995, Karl Malone recorded 42 points on nearly 70% shooting in a tight win over the Indiana Pacers.

For the eighth time in his career, Karl Malone was selected to play in the All-Star Game. That February was Malone's best month for individual performance. He scored 30 or more points in 11 of 17 games, with 10 double-doubles. As the season was winding down, Malone scored 45 points in their third-to-the-last regular season game. It was in a 19-point win against the Houston Rockets. He also had 17 rebounds and 5 assists in that game.

For the 1994-95 regular season, Karl Malone averaged 26.7 points, 10.6 rebounds, 3.5 assists, and 1.6 steals while shooting over 53% from the field. He was once again a member of the All-NBA First Team as he further solidified his claim to be one of the top five best players in the NBA.

Malone led the Jazz to a franchise best 60-win season on their way to the playoffs as the third seed in the West.

In the first round of the playoffs, however, they met the defending champions Houston Rockets with Hakeem Olajuwon playing inspired basketball. The Jazz won Game 1 by merely 2 points, thanks to 25 points and 14 rebounds from The Mailman. Houston took Game 2 behind 7 three-pointers by Kenny Smith. In Game 3, Karl Malone delivered 32 points, 19 rebounds, and 5 assists to lead the Utah Jazz to a 13-point win. Despite being one game away from proceeding to the second round, the Jazz faltered. Houston took Games 4 and 5 despite back-to-back 30 point outputs by Karl Malone. The Rockets eventually proceeded to the NBA finals and successfully defended their title.

## More Conference Finals Woes

The 1995-1996 season brought in rewards for Malone, though not with the Jazz. It was with the United States basketball team at the Atlanta Olympic Games that Malone would see success. He chipped in around 8 points a game and the USA won gold once more.

It was also that in that season that Michael Jordan played a full season after returning from retirement. In the time when Jordan was retired, there was every reason to believe that Karl Malone was the best player in the NBA. But, with MJ back, the quest for an NBA title got a little tougher than in the previous two seasons.

Nevertheless, at 32 years old, Karl Malone was still a beast. He kept himself in top shape every single year. His conditioning allowed him to play almost every game of the season, and he looked younger and more athletic than players a decade younger than he was. Fitness was something other players take for granted. But that was Malone's bread and butter. That was what made him a dangerous player deep into his 30s.

Malone started the season with nine double-doubles in his first 20 outings. He scored below 20 points in only three games in that stretch. On December 7, 1995, Karl grabbed 22 rebounds against the Denver Nuggets. Just a game after that loss to the Nuggets, The Mailman delivered an amazing 51-point performance in a win against the Golden State Warriors. In that game, he sank 19 of 28 from the field and 13 of 16 from the foul stripe. At 32 years old, Karl Malone was still capable of a 50-point game.

On December 26, he had another great outing, with 47 points against the Portland Trailblazers. He shot 21 of 31 from the floor in that 10-point win. His third game with 40 or more points came against the Detroit Pistons on January 29, 1996, when he had 40 points and 10 rebounds in a 9-point win. Barely a week later, he scored 39 in a tough loss to the Lakers. Malone was an All-Star for the ninth straight season. Karl then renewed his contract with the Jazz despite not seeing a lot of playoff success with the team. The man was loyal as anyone could be.

Karl Malone averaged 25.7 points (the lowest since his second season), 9.8 rebounds (the lowest since his rookie year), 4.2 rebounds, and 1.7 steals for the season. He played all 82 games and averaged 38 minutes per outing. He was named to the All-NBA First Team for the eighth straight season. At 32 years old, most star players would play fewer games and minutes to preserve them for a deep playoff run. But Karl was a freak of nature. He did not need to play fewer minutes to be in top shape during the postseason. Karl Malone was in a class of his own when you talk about fitness, endurance, and conditioning. He led the Jazz to the third seed in the league with a record of 55-27.

Karl Malone continued tearing up inside the paint in the first round of the playoffs against the Portland Trailblazers. His team won Games 1 and 2, when he scored 33 and 30 points, respectively. Despite a 35-point output in Game 3, Malone and his team lost the game by only 3 points. The Blazers limited the superstar power forward to merely 15 points in Game 4 as they took that one to force Game 5. The Utah Jazz returned to top form and completely devastated the Blazers by 38 points in the closeout game.

Against the higher-seeded San Antonio Spurs, the Jazz did not seem affected by the Spurs' home-court advantage. They beat their foes in Game 1 by 20 points. Malone had 23 in that game. The Spurs took revenge by winning Game 2. With Malone scoring 32 points and pulling down 11 boards in Game 3, Utah won by 30 points. They then routed the Spurs in Game 4 by 15. Though San Antonio inched closer by winning Game 5, the Jazz wrapped things up with a 27-point victory in Game 6. Malone had 25 points, 13 rebounds, and 6 assists in that clinching game.

The Utah Jazz faced the top-seeded Seattle SuperSonics in their third overall conference finals appearance. The Jazz were routed by Seattle in a devastating 30-point loss. Malone was limited to 21 that game. Though Karl had a bounce-back performance in Game 2, the Sonics took that one by 4 points. When the series shifted over to Utah for Game 3, Malone had 28 points and 18 rebounds to secure a 20-point win for his team. However, the Sonics won Game 4 by 2 points to take command of the series, 3-1.

At that point, the Jazz were merely one loss away from yet another conference finals loss. They showed a lot of intestinal fortitude in the next two games. In Seattle, the Jazz inched a game closer, winning Game 5 by 3 points, thanks to the 29 points and 15 rebounds of Malone. In Game 6, Karl had 32 points, 10 rebounds, 7 assists, and 4 steals in a 35-point annihilation of the SuperSonics. Though they forced Game 7, the Jazz lost a close game that would have given the franchise its first NBA finals appearance.

# First MVP Season, First Finals Appearance

The 1996-97 was a season of firsts for the Utah Jazz. It was one of the best seasons not only in franchise history but also in the history of the NBA. Byron Russell, who played barely 10 minutes a game in the previous season, rose to become a good starter because of his defensive abilities and his outside shooting. The team also gave the starting center spot to a young 7'2" bull of a center named Greg Ostertag. The improvements to those role players, along with the steady play of the core superstars, led to the Jazz's improved season.

At 33 years old, Karl Malone was still a force to be reckoned with, as he was still one of the best players in the NBA despite an influx of a lot of talented youngsters. Karl led the Jazz to victory in 17 of their first 20 games. He had 13 double-doubles in that span of games; 10 of those double-doubles came in victories. He also scored 30 or more points seven times while scoring fewer than 20 points merely thrice. There was no doubt that Malone was the driving force behind a great start for the Utah Jazz.

On January 22, 1997, Karl Malone scored 41 points on 16 of 28 shooting from the field in a 12-point win against the Phoenix Suns. After playing in the All-Star Game for the 10th straight time, Malone scored 30 or more points in six straight games. He then had 41 in a March 3 victory versus the Golden State Warriors. From March up to April, Karl Malone led the Utah Jazz to 15 straight victories. All but three of those wins were by double digits. That was how great the Jazz were that season. Of course, they would not get to that point without their Mailman, who always delivered when needed.

Karl Malone averaged 27.4 points, 9.9 rebounds, 4.5 assists, and 1.4 steals that season. He had 43 double-doubles, including a triple-double game against the Toronto Raptors, in which he had 32 points, 13 rebounds, and 10 assists. Karl also shot 55% from the field as he scored over any player defending him. It was also during that season that Malone surpassed the 25,000-point and 10,000-rebound mark. He was merely the fifth player in NBA history at that time to reach those two marks.

As he led the team to a franchise record 64 wins, Karl Malone was named the 1997 NBA Most Valuable Player. A 12-year veteran at 33 years old, Malone was the oldest player to win the award for the first time. He was once again an All-NBA First Team member and was named to the All-Defensive First Team for the very first time in his career. It was certainly by far his best season as a professional.

The Utah Jazz also had the best season in franchise history. In the first round, they stormed past the Los Angeles Clippers with an easy three-game sweep. Malone had double-doubles in all of those three wins. His best outing for that series was a 39-point, 11-rebound performance in Game 2, which they won by 6 points. Games 1 and 3 were both blowouts.

In the second round, they faced the much-improved Los Angeles Lakers, led by new acquisition Shaquille O'Neal. In that series, the Jazz put the defensive clamps on Shaq, who was coming off a demolition job in a series against the Blazers in the first round. The Jazz won Game 1 by denying O'Neal and by banking on the double-double performance of Karl Malone. Though Game 2 was a close fight, the Jazz still came out of that one with a win, thanks to the 31 points, 11 rebounds, and 5 assists of their MVP.

In Game 3, Malone played arguably the worst playoff game he ever had. He was 2 of 20 from the field for 15 points, and the Lakers came out with a 20-point win. Malone made up for his sorry performance in Game 4, when he exploded for 42 points to lead the Jazz to a 15-point win. He had another stellar performance in Game 5. The Mailman scored 32 points and delivered 20 rebounds in an overtime win that saw the Jazz march to the Western Conference finals with a win.

In the West Finals, Utah faced a Houston Rockets team that was led by three future Hall of Fame players, Hakeem Olajuwon, Clyde Drexler, and Charles Barkley, who was one of the best power forwards of that era alongside Malone. But the Jazz had Stockton and Malone, two players who were arguably the best at their positions in that decade. Games 1 and 2 weren't even close as Utah won both by double digits. Malone had double-double performances in both games.

In the Rockets' home court, the Jazz stumbled in Games 3 and 4. Malone was limited to merely 21 points in each game. Though that number is normally enough for any player, it was not the best performances for the MVP. The Jazz bounced back in Games 5 and 6. They won both close games, thanks to the double-double exploits of The Mailman. As the Utah Jazz team dispatched the Rockets in six games, they were going to a place where no Jazz team had ever gone before—the NBA finals.

Malone had constantly finished second in scoring to Jordan throughout his career, but he was determined not to finish second to him in the NBA finals. The talk of the nation was about the NBA finals, where the previous two MVPs squared off on the court. Michael Jordan and Karl Malone were arguably the two best players of that era. It was a match made in heaven, as the two legendary greats squared off for the richest prize of basketball.

Jordan and his Bulls took Games 1 and 2—games in which Malone struggled, going 6 for 20 from the field at one point. Karl could not get past the tough defense of Dennis Rodman. He had 23 points in Game 1 and 20 in Game 2.

The Jazz were not known for lying down and taking it, though; they rallied back and won both Games 3 and 4 on their home floor. This time, Malone excelled, as he scored 37 points in the third game. He then had 23 in Game 4, which saw the Jazz win due to an out-of-this-world assist pass by Stockton to Malone for a game-winning layup. Struggles returned to haunt Malone, though, as he found it hard to score from the foul line or even from the field against the Bulls' swarming defense. Ultimately, the Bulls took Games 5 and 6 to win the NBA championship.

## Back to the Finals, Rematch with Jordan and the Bulls

The domination of the league at the hands of the Jazz continued into the next season. They proved to everyone in the league that their historical 1996-97 was not a fluke and that they could still continue to play at a high level with their capable core. Though their dominant duo was already aging, they were still arguably the best pick-and-roll combo in the whole league.

At 34 years old, Karl Malone continued to pile up numbers beyond what a player his age was supposed to be capable of. To start the 1997-98 season, The Mailman scored 20 or more points 28 times through his first 30 games. He had 18 double-double performances in those games. He even had a 42-point, 18-rebound outing in a win against the LA Clippers. Malone was the personification of the saying "age is just a number." What's more amazing was that Karl Malone had to do it without Stockton early in the season because his partner was recovering from knee surgery.

As soon as the new year started, Malone went on a personal tear: a 29-game streak of scoring 20 or more points. In the midst of all that, Karl Malone was selected to play in his 11th straight All-Star Game that season. He also scored 40 points in a win against the Milwaukee Bucks on March 7, 1998. In the following game, he grabbed 21 rebounds against the Houston Rockets.

In an amazing effort for a man in the middle of his 30s, Karl Malone scored 56 points on April 7 in a win over the Golden State Warriors. He went 18 of 29 from the field and 19 of 23 from the free throw line. After that performance, he still had enough left in the tank, as he scored 30 or more points in back-to-back games before wrapping things up with a 44-point performance in a win against the Minnesota Timberwolves and the young Kevin Garnett

Karl averaged 27 points, 10.3 rebounds, 3.9 assists, and 1.2 steals in his 13th NBA season. Malone's 27-point average and outstanding season would have won him his second MVP award in a world in which Michael Jordan did not exist. Malone had now lost a golden chance at an elusive championship and a second MVP award that he rightfully deserved. Nevertheless, he was All-NBA First Team for the 10th straight season. All this proved to be an incentive for The Mailman to work overtime and deliver in the playoffs like never before.

Though the Jazz started the first round losing two out of the first three games against the Houston Rockets, they closed out the series in Games 4 and 5, thanks to the combined 60-point, 28-rebound output that Malone poured in to power his team to the second round. In the second round, Karl schooled the rookie Tim Duncan as he and his team defeated the future Hall-of-Famer's San Antonio Spurs in five games. Karl did not have the best series in that five-game stretch versus the Spurs, but he did just enough to have his team advancing to the Western Conference finals.

The Jazz faced the Los Angeles Lakers in the Conference finals. Led by Shaq in his prime, and the much-improved teenage Kobe Bryant, the Lakers were supposed to be one of the toughest matchups for the Jazz. However, it was the other way around. Malone tore the Lakers to shreds in that series. Utah won Game 1 by 35, where Malone had 29 points and 10 boards. He then scored 33 in another win in Game 2. The Jazz routed the Lakers in the next two games, with the superstar power forward scoring 26 and 32.

The Malone-Jordan rematch did not play out quite the same way it had the year before. The Jazz took the first game at the Delta Center 88-85, with Malone racking up 21 points and 14 rebounds despite a tough shooting night. Chicago fought right back, though, winning Game 2 by 3. They then routed the Jazz by 42 points in Game 3 before winning Game 4 by 4 points. The Bulls seemed to have the

Jazz's number in those three wins in which the defensive pairing of Dennis Rodman and Scottie Pippen shut down Malone to unheard-of effect. With the Jazz looking at certain doom, Malone played harder in the fifth game and put up 39 points, 9 rebounds, and 5 assists in an 83-81 win in Chicago. The Mailman had a 17 for 27 shooting night. He also had 9 rebounds, 5 assists, and only 1 turnover. The stage was set for Game 6.

If there is one defining image that separates people who are NBA fans and those who are not, it comes from this game. The Jazz blew out the Bulls through the first three quarters, but practically walked off the court and let the Bulls play against imaginary defenders as they breeze their way back into the game. There were barely 19 seconds left, and the Jazz had an 86-85 lead, on their way to tie up the series at three games apiece and heading to Salt Lake City for Game 7. Malone is open and the ball is passed to him—but it's turned over, stolen by—you guessed it—Michael Jordan. The clock read 5.2 seconds left, and Jordan completes his greatest, most defining moment. He jumps, shoots, and the ball goes where it always went when Jordan shot it—

through the net. The Bulls won 87-86 to wrap up the team's second three-peat in a span of less than a decade.

## Slow Fall Out of Title Contention

Michael Jordan retired for the second time after winning his second three-peat and his sixth NBA title. What that meant was that the NBA was guaranteed new champions. What that also meant was that Karl Malone and his squad had one less problem without Jordan. Normally, the Jazz would have been the title favorites for that season as the second powerhouse team of the 1990s was significantly weakened. However, it was also at that time when other Western Conference teams began to rise.

The San Antonio Spurs, with reigning Rookie of the Year Tim Duncan playing alongside the dominant David Robinson, were quickly rising in the West, as their twin towers were a force to be reckoned with. The other team that had a legitimate chance of dethroning the reigning Western Conference kings was the Los Angeles Lakers. Shaquille O'Neal was just entering his prime while the young Kobe Bryant was quickly improving, gaining confidence, and molding into his superstar potential. It seemed like the Western Conference would not be as smooth as in previous years.

The 1998-99 season did not start until February of 1999 because of a labor dispute between the players union and the team owners. When the dispute was finally settled, it was already February, and the season had to be shortened to 50 games. That was sort of a good thing for older teams like the Jazz. Karl Malone and John Stockton needed to rest their bones after two straight deep playoff runs. A shortened season was what the doctor ordered for them as they began their quest for an NBA title in the post-Michael Jordan era.

Karl Malone continued to defy age that season as he led the Jazz all year long. In the 49 games that he played, Malone had 22 double-doubles, including a triple-double in the final regular season game. Karl had 29 points, 12 rebounds, and 10 assists in a big win against the Clippers on May 4. He scored 30 or more points 10 times, as he averaged 23.8 points, 9.4 rebounds, and 4.1 assists. For the second time in his career, Karl Malone was voted the league's Most Valuable Player. He was also First Team All-NBA for the

11ᵗʰ consecutive year. However, his All-Star streak was cut because the 1999 season did not feature a midseason classic due to schedule constraints. The Jazz finished as the third seed in the West by winning 37 of their 50 outings.

In the first round of the 1999 playoffs, Malone and company ran up against the Sacramento Kings, another rising team in the West. While the Jazz won Game 1 away by 30 points despite a poor shooting performance by Malone, the Kings took Games 2 and 3 in spite of double-double games by The Mailman. Malone had 21 points and 16 rebounds to tie the series up in Game 4. In Game 5, he struggled to 20 points as his team advanced to the second round with a tough series against the Kings.

In the second round, they faced the defensive-minded Portland Trailblazers. Matched up against the young and physical Rasheed Wallace, Malone helped the Jazz win Game 1 with his 25 points and 12 rebounds. However, Portland found ways to stifle the aging Jazz offense. Malone barely got shots up in Games 2 to 4, as the Blazers won three straight outings to the dismay of the Jazz. In Game 5, Utah finally got a break, winning by 17. However,

Portland defended Karl Malone, who shot 3 out of 16 for 8 points in Game 6, as they proceeded to the Western Conference finals with a 12-point win. With that Utah loss, the West was guaranteed new champions.

With the San Antonio Spurs winning the NBA title in 1999 and with the Los Angeles Lakers improving mightily, the Utah Jazz were quickly forgotten as a great team despite a steady 1999-2000 season. The rise of younger and fresher power forwards like Duncan, Webber, and Garnett also helped the world forget that Malone had dominated that position for more than a decade. But Malone's individual performances that season made the world realize that The Mailman still owned the title as the best power forward in the NBA.

Karl started the season scoring 20 or more in eight of his first 10 outings. In his 10th game, he scored 40 points on 17 out of 25 shooting against the Milwaukee Bucks. He had 12 double-doubles in his first 20 games. From December 1999 to January 2000, Malone had 16 straight games of scoring 20 or more points. He also had seven double-doubles in that stretch.

As he began to show the world that he was still a dominating force at the age of 36, Karl Malone was selected to his 12th All-Star Game appearance. He averaged 25.5 points, 9.5 rebounds, and 3.7 assists while playing 36 minutes in all 82 games. He was named to the All-NBA Second Team as he led the Jazz to the second seed with a 55-27 record.

Malone started the playoffs on the highest note possible. He scored 50 points against the Seattle SuperSonics in an 11-point win in Game 1. You rarely see 36-year-old players scoring 50 points in the regular season, and it's even rarer in the playoffs because of the tougher defense. The Mailman needed to deliver only 23 points in Game 2, as the Jazz won by 14. However, the Sonics bounced back on their own floor, winning both Games 3 and 4 by 11 points. In Game 5, Malone delivered 27 points to help his team close out the tough Sonics squad.

In the second round, the Utah Jazz met the Portland Trailblazers once again. Though the league was already without Michael Jordan, his partner-in-crime Scottie Pippen was still lurking around. Worse, he was playing in

Portland that season. The Jazz continued their woes against a remnant of the 1990s Bulls team as Portland took Games 1, 2, and 3 by 19, 18, and 19 respectively. It seemed as if the Blazers had Utah's number. Malone's struggles against the Portland defense continued. The Jazz won Game 4, but it was all academic, as the Trailblazers took Game 5 to advance to the conference finals.

Karl Malone continued to carry the Utah Jazz on his wide shoulders in the 2001-02 season. At that time, his buddy John Stockton was showing signs of aging as he was incapable of the feats he used to do a few years back. But Malone was different. He was still putting up numbers not even 20-year olds could not achieve.

As a 37-year old, Karl Malone started the season scoring 20 or more in his first six games. He had three 30-point outings in that stretch. On December 20, 2000, Malone delivered 41 points and 13 rebounds in a win against the Philadelphia 76ers. He was selected as an All-Star for the 13th time in his career. With averages of 23.2 points, 8.3 rebounds, and 4.5 assists, Karl Malone was named to the All-NBA Third Team, his 14th overall and last All-NBA selection. He led the Jazz to a 53-29 record, which was good enough for the fourth seed in the West.

Matched up against a young Dirk Nowitzki of the Dallas Mavericks, Malone's experience initially triumphed over the youth of the big German. He led the Jazz to wins in both Games 1 and 2 while averaging 30 points. However, youth triumphed in the long term. Nowitzki had 33 in Game 3 to burn the older Malone and lead the Mavs to a win. Malone, again, could not stop the 7-foot German from scoring 33 in a Game 4 loss for the Jazz. As Game 5 settled down to be close, it was Dallas that came out the victors by 1 point.

Though the Utah Jazz had suffered another disappointing loss in the playoffs, their 2001-02 offseason would get a little bit brighter thanks to the acquisition of Russian forward Andrei Kirilenko, who was drafted with the 24th pick in the 2001 NBA Draft. Other than that, the team maintained the aging core. They were still banking on Stockton and Malone even after all those years.

Malone, for his part, did not disappoint. At 38 years old, he was still balling like he was 28. He would put to shame guys more than a decade younger than he was. In the month of November alone, Karl Malone had three games with 30 or more points. He had six double-doubles in that month. He had his season high of 39 points in a win against the Golden State Warriors on December 8, 2001.

At the end of another All-Star season, Karl Malone had averaged 22.4 points, 8.6 rebounds, 4.3 assists, and 1.9 steals. For the first time since 1988, Malone was not a member of an All-NBA Team. Nonetheless, The Mailman was still delivering better than most other young power forwards in the league at that time. He led the Utah Jazz to a mediocre 44-38 finish, but they still qualified for the playoffs as the eighth seed in the West. In a disappointing first-round performance, Karl Malone and his Jazz were easily ousted by the top-seeded Sacramento Kings in four games.

## Final Season with the Jazz

The 2002-03 season was almost identical to their previous year's campaign. Though they were bolstered by Matt

Harpring, a wing shooter, the main duo of Stockton and Malone was not getting any younger. In fact, Stockton was already 40 years old, while The Mailman was not far behind at 39. Despite that, they were still a mighty combo for the Jazz.

In that season, Malone began to show signs that he was finally slowing down as an NBA great. In his first 20 games, Karl did not score more than 30 points. In fact, he even had zero-point output in his fourth game, which was against the Seattle SuperSonics. In December, after seven games of scoring less than 20 points, Karl Malone broke out with a 31-point output in a close win against the Houston Rockets. He then put up 34 points in January of 2003, and he scored 40 points in a win against the Orlando Magic on March 12.

Karl Malone averaged 20.6 points, 7.8 rebounds, and 4.7 assists for the season. Not too shabby for a man nearing 40 years old. Even after such an amazing output, Karl was not an All-Star that season. Nevertheless, it was during that season that Karl Malone would move up the list of career scorers in the NBA. With a total of 36,374 career points, he passed Wilt Chamberlain and became the player with the second most points in NBA history. Malone was trailing only Kareem Abdul-Jabbar in that regard. He led the Utah Jazz to 47 wins, and they made the playoffs as the seventh seed in the ultra-competitive Western Conference. Matched up once again with the Sacramento Kings, the Jazz lost in five games. In the inaugural postseason with a seven-game first-round series, Malone seemed a shell of his former self, as he averaged 19.6 points on 40.5% shooting against the Kings.

When the whole season ended, John Stockton decided to call it a career. Stockton was the one responsible for creating open looks for Malone. He made it easier for Karl to score even as he was nearing his 40s. Stockton retired with career averages of 13.1 points and 10.5 assists. He finished with a career total of 15,806 dimes, which is top all time in career assists by a player. Stockton is arguably the second-best pure point guard ever to play the game. After Stockton's retirement, Malone had contemplated hanging up the sneakers. But, as a free agent, he saw an opportunity to join the Los Angeles Lakers in an attempt to win an NBA title. He took it.

## Final Season, Laker Year, Retirement

With only one major achievement eluding him, The Mailman looked to the best chance he had to win a championship: the Los Angeles Lakers, who had won three of the last four NBA titles. Joining with Kobe Bryant, Shaq, and the aging Gary Payton, Malone pulled on the gold and purple jersey that he had played against for so long. The team was not the only change for Malone—the number 32 that he had worn in Utah was retired for Magic Johnson in Los Angeles and, despite his former Dream Team teammate telling him he could wear it, Karl chose to wear number 11.

Karl Malone was not used to playing behind other teammates. As a Laker, he was playing third fiddle to Shaquille O'Neal in his prime, and Kobe Bryant, who was still improving as a superstar. Though Malone was just a role player with the Spurs, he played his role very well. Karl scored in double digits in each of his first 23 games as a Laker.

Things started out well for the Lakers, who were predicted to win the title that year. However, in December, Malone injured his knee and did not return until late in the season. He made his return on March 12, 2004. He scored 13 in that game. Malone played admirably for a 40-year old as the season ended. He helped the Lakers win the second seed in the powerful Western Conference. In that season, Karl Malone averaged 13.2 points, 8.7 rebounds, and 3.9 assists. He played 42 games that season. The 40 games he missed was more than he had missed in his entire career with the Jazz.

The mighty Lakers routed the Houston Rockets in five games. Malone had a flashback performance in Game 4, scoring 30 points and grabbing 13 rebounds. He then had 18 in the closeout game. The Lakers were suddenly seeing classic Mailman in those two games.

Karl played his part in the second round of the 2004 playoffs, defending the San Antonio Spurs' Tim Duncan and not scoring more than 13 points the entire series. The Mailman focused on the defensive end as he gave the scoring duties to the transcendent Shaq and Kobe combo.

Using his large body, Malone pushed Duncan around to make life difficult for the man regarded as the best power forward at that time (and possibly of all time). Although the Lakers lost the two opening games, they went on to win four straight on their way to the conference finals.

In the West Finals, they met the top-seeded Minnesota Timberwolves, led by the MVP Kevin Garnett, who was also regarded as a contender for the title of best power forward in that era. Malone would do his part in trying to make life difficult for KG. He put so much focus on the defensive end that in his two best scoring games of the series he put up 17 points, in a Game 1 win and in a Game 5 loss. The Lakers disposed of the Wolves in six games and they were on their way to another NBA finals appearance.

It looked good for The Mailman to finally win his first NBA championship—but the Detroit Pistons had other plans. Malone injured his knee again and played injured through the first four games of the series. Despite his best efforts, he was unable to feature anymore after that. He was reduced to watching his dream crumble before him yet again when the Pistons won the series in five by defending Shaq and Kobe physically and admirably.

During the offseason, Malone had knee surgery to repair the damage done to his aging body the season before. However, things turned ugly between Karl and the Lakers superstar Kobe Bryant. Kobe and Malone, along with their wives, had been good friends during The Mailman's tenure in Los Angeles. However, it was reported that Bryant's wife Vanessa asked Malone, "What are you hunting, cowboy?" one day when she saw that he was wearing a cowboy hat and boots. Malone supposedly replied "Little Mexican girls," referencing Vanessa's age (18) and her ethnicity. Malone decided to leave the Lakers following this feud with Kobe, telling *USA Today*: "This is a Hollywood soap opera, and I am not going to be a star in another Bryant soap opera."

It was rumored then that Malone would join either the Knicks or the Spurs. However, Malone found himself at the Delta Center in Salt Lake City. This time, it was not to sign a contract or pull on the purple and blue jersey. Instead, he was leading a press conference in February

2005 announcing his retirement from the game after 19 seasons.

"I look at basketball as 100 percent physically and 100 percent mentally. And if I cannot bring you 200 percent, from me, I cannot bring you anything," Malone said. He was still physically fit to play the game but, after a long career, there was not any more desire to play another season of professional basketball. After almost two decades of playing professional basketball, Karl Malone finished his career with 36,928 total points, which still stand as the second most in NBA history. He was an All-Star and an All-NBA selection 14 times. As decorated as his career was, the only thing that eluded him was an NBA championship.

# Chapter 5: Malone's Personal Life

On December 24, 1990, Karl Malone married Kay Kinsey, who had been the Miss Idaho pageant winner in 1988. Together, the two shared many of the same passions such as pro wrestling, hunting, tractor pulls, and trucking. Together, the Malones have three daughters (Kadee, Kylee, and Karlee) and one son (Karl Jr.). The family was the exact picture of strength and warmth that Malone always wanted. His son Karl Jr. played football for Cedar Creek High School in Ruston, Louisiana, and committed to LSU in 2013.

Though The Mailman may have delivered on the court, there are those who would say he did not do so as a man. During his career, he was faced with two paternity lawsuits by women he had known in Summerfield. Between Bonita Ford and Gloria Bell, Malone has three illegitimate children.

Malone was 17 when Ford, also 17, gave birth to twins Daryl and Cheryl. By 1998, Malone accepted paternity of the Ford twins and became heavily involved in their lives.

Cheryl was well noted for following in her biological father's footsteps. She attended Summerfield High School and Louisiana Tech and played basketball at both schools. Cheryl chose to wear the number 32 and was drafted in 2003 by the Detroit Shock of the WNBA. Malone has been seen in attendance at a few of her games over the years.

While he made an effort to be in the lives of the Ford twins, the case is not the same for Demetress Bell. Malone was a 20-year-old sophomore at Louisiana Tech, but Bell's mother Gloria was only 13 when she gave birth to the Dallas Cowboys offensive tackle. Malone never confirmed to the public that Bell is his son, but blood work has shown that there is 99% likelihood that Malone or even one of his brothers is the father. Bell never learned of Malone's parentage until he was in high school because his mother did not want him to be upset over the NBA star's refusal to be in his life. It is reported that Malone and Bell have only ever spoken once in the latter's life. Bell claims that Malone told him that he would have to make his own way in life because it was "too late for [Malone] to be [Bell's] father." Despite his relationship with Malone, or lack of one, Bell is close with the Ford twins, who acknowledge him as being their brother and a part of the family.

While Bell's mother was only 13 at the time of Demetress' birth, the family decided not to pursue criminal charges against The Mailman. Their thinking was that there was no possible way for Malone to provide for Demetress if the former was in jail. During the lawsuit, the case was settled out of court for a large lump sum paid to Gloria Bell after Malone deemed that $125 a week in child support was "too much." However, no other form of support, either fatherly or financially, was ever given to Demetress.

This lack of fatherhood is somewhat curious for Malone, given that he was fatherless himself and one would think that he would not wish that upon one of his own children. It is also curious because of the amount of work that Malone and his wife Kay do with sick children on behalf of the Karl Malone Foundation for Kids. In 2003, Utah Governor Mike Leavitt presented Karl and Kay with a special declaration because of their "incredible service, friendship, and generosity to the state of Utah." It is because of acts like those that make his absence from

Bell's life strange. Others speculate that if Cheryl had not attended the same schools that her father did and there was not so much attention drawn to her following in her father's footsteps, Malone might not be present in her life.

Malone always had a dream of owning and driving a big rig truck. In March 1993 he made this dream a reality—starting up a six-rig fleet named Malone Enterprises. The company only lasted two years due to Malone's limited involvement because of his basketball career and competition in the industry. Malone still drives his favorite truck, though, a $190,000 rig painted with a panorama of the Old West painted on it. Malone is also the owner of a 52-acre ranch in El Dorado, Arkansas, where he is a beef master cattle breeder. On this ranch, animals such as cattle can go for as much as $200,000 each.

Malone is a man of many hats indeed. In fact, he has served on the Board of Directors for the National Rifle Association (NRA). He also contributed $4,000 to George W. Bush's campaign for re-election as President in 2004. Currently, The Mailman owns an Arby's and a Teriyaki Grill in Ruston, Louisiana. He has also been an assistant coach for the Louisiana Tech basketball team and in May of 2013 he returned to the Utah Jazz as a big man coach.

# Chapter 6: Impact on Basketball

Over the 19 years that Malone played professionally in the NBA, he showed again and again that he was the single most dominant power forward in the league during the time he played. His work ethic and his ability to stay in shape constantly gave him an advantage over the other players around him. He was always willing to work harder than anyone else, which is why he won two MVP awards, was nominated to the NBA First Team 11 times, and was named to the All-Defensive Team three times.

His body builder state of mind was the reason that he proved so durable throughout his career. Even during his later years, Malone was able to play game after game. He missed games only through suspension or injury, and the injuries occurred only during the last season of his career, with the Lakers. The way he built himself has been seen as an inspiration for players who want to be at the top of their physical game. The way that he worked himself during the offseason showed how determined and serious he was. He can be seen as a role model because of the way he never dwelled on mistakes and didn't let his errors defeat him. Instead, he saw these mistakes as a way of learning, propelling him forward so that he knew where he could improve and do better the next time he was on the court.

Because of his ability to keep his body in shape and be in top conditioning form, Karl Malone was always ready to score more than 20 points a game in almost every season he's played. Even when he was in his late 30s, Malone was still a lot better than 95% of all the other power forwards in the league. He could put a 24-year-old to shame with his ability to score and rebound at an advanced age. Because of his ability to stay healthy, Karl Malone has consistently played 82 games per season. That helped him score the number of points he accumulated in his career. He's certainly a freak of nature as far as health is concerned. How does that impact the game of basketball? Well, it only means that a good physique, together with a lot of skill and conditioning, can take your NBA career deeper than the average one.

Over the course of his career, Malone constantly struggled from the foul line. His free throws were the shots he could never bank on. However, during his later veteran years, he improved his free throw percentage from 50% to 70%. If free throws were a mountain, they were just one more that Malone had to climb and reach the top of in his life. He was never a stranger to obstacles, he overcame each one as they reared their head and greeted him like an old friend.

# Chapter 7: Karl Malone's Legacy and Future

In 2010, Karl "The Mailman" Malone was inducted into the Naismith Memorial Basketball Hall of Fame alongside Scottie Pippen and the members of the Dream Team from 1992, which Larry Bird stopped just short of calling the "greatest basketball team ever assembled." There was no speech more laden with emotion than that of Malone's. "I am here because of her," he said, referring to his mother Shirley, who passed away seven years before her son's induction.

He went on to thank the Utah Jazz owner Larry Miller for believing in him from the very beginning, when no other team in the 1985 draft did. Malone went on to say that his success came from his staying true to his roots. "I hope I did it the way my peers did it before me," Malone said. "I did not do anything but try to play hard."

There is tremendous truth in Malone's statement. While other basketball greats such as Larry Bird and Magic Johnson got by throughout their careers with amazing skill,

Malone made up for natural skill by working harder than anyone else. Sadly, it's the lack of that talent and an NBA championship that causes people to look back at the career Malone had and label him as "not that great." People such as the aforementioned Bird and Johnson could have their bad games forgotten because they were truly great. However, the failures that Malone had when it truly mattered always seem to make his constant excellence not matter so much. The career of Karl Malone shows us that we forget about a lot of great years because we only remember the few best ones.

The "Mailman" nickname was given to Malone because he was constant in delivering good performances. He earned that back when he was in college. That meant that Karl Malone had already been delivering at a high level even in the earlier parts of his basketball career. Consistency surrounded the Jazz throughout Malone's tenure with the team. Everything became guaranteed when Malone led the team from Salt Lake City: He would score 27 points, Stockton and he would nail the pick-and-roll offense, and the Jazz would win 50 or more games a season and then crash out of the playoffs to the Rockets or lose to the Bulls in the finals.

Karl Malone may be the hardest working professional basketball player in history. No pro player today works as hard off the ball as they do on it. There are many egos and great concerns of shoe sponsorships, but those troubles never got to Malone. He was only concerned with being the best that he could be. He worked hard getting rebounds when the opposing team missed a shot; he linked up with John Stockton and dished the ball out to his teammates.

When things were not working for him, he worked hard to adjust them—no matter if these adjustments were not noticeable on a large scale. On and off the court, there isn't a single player that has worked harder than Karl Malone. No one hears about players bailing hay and wrestling hogs in the sweltering heat and humidity of Louisiana. No, modern players prefer the air conditioning and benefits of a gym membership. These are the same modern players who don't run their bodies into the dirt going back to defend, the same modern players who value scoring points over assists and rebounds—the "little statistics" that casual fans don't particularly care about.

The pick-and-roll offense that the Jazz employed with Stockton and Malone was never one for scoring in transition, apart from a dunk. In spite of this, Malone was nailing in shot after shot on the pick-and-roll. That was the way he catapulted himself up the scoring lists—different from how anyone else would do it because he could do it better. Lay-ups and shots from the mid-range propelled Malone into being the most dominant power forward in the game. Sure, he did not ever win the big one. How can we let that one fact allow the world to deny the constant greatness that Karl Malone gave night after night? He paved the way for the future of the power forward position in the NBA and all of basketball.

No, he did not have grace or sweet moves like so many other players of the time or the players of the current generation. Malone showed that grace isn't required to be successful. No flashy moves? Okay, but there he was each night finishing consistently with 50% or higher shooting, 27 points, and 8 or 9 rebounds. It was all a routine for him, he went out night after night to do his job and help his team win games the way that he knew how to do. There is greatness within blue collar workers who will never be revered the same way that celebrities are—workers who go out and run themselves into the ground to ensure the right result.

Because of everything he's achieved as a player, there is no doubt in anyone's mind that he is the best ever to have played for the Salt Lake City NBA team. With a career total of 36,374 points for the Utah Jazz, he is by far the best scorer the franchise has ever seen. Who finished second? Why, it's none other than his buddy John Stockton with 19,711 points. Malone also finished with 14,601 career rebounds for the Jazz. That's almost 8,000 more than Mark Eaton, who finished second behind him in career boards. Even as a power forward, Malone is second only to John Stockton in career steals and assists as a Jazz. Finally, with over 53,000 minutes for Utah, nobody has ever given more sweat and blood for the Jazz team. Even though he had multiple opportunities to leave Utah in his prime, Malone never did so. He was loyalty personified. He was the Utah Jazz personified.

We know Karl's place in the long history of the Utah Jazz. But, where does he belong in the annals of NBA history. As a power forward, Karl Malone has long been regarded as the best at that position. He dominated that role ever since he made his rookie debut. From the late 1980s up to the latter part of the 1990s, Karl Malone was the best power forward in the NBA. He proved it by being named to the All-NBA First Team for 11 straight seasons. How did he do it? With a steady diet of skill and conditioning, Malone kept himself healthy and in top shape every single night. Despite playing a physical brand of basketball, he stayed away from injury. By doing so, he outplayed every other power forward of his era. He even ran up against the golden generation of power forwards as he faced the younger versions of Tim Duncan, Dirk Nowitzki, and Kevin Garnett.

However, Malone's inability to win an NBA title has had people doubting his place as the best power forward to have ever played the game. Tim Duncan as now been considered as the best to have ever played that position. Duncan has won five NBA titles, which is five more than Malone. Even great power forwards such as Garnett and Nowitzki have won titles. But nobody could ever blame The Mailman for not being able to deliver a title to Utah. Blame Michael Jordan. A lot of greats that played in the 1990s never got to win a title because of Jordan. You could mention names such as Charles Barkley, Reggie Miller, and Patrick Ewing. Those players, like Malone, were just unlucky to have gone up against Jordan in his prime. Karl's inability to win an NBA title was not so much his fault even if he is regarded as the second-best player behind Jordan in the 1990 era. Because of that, you can never disregard his place as one of the greatest power forwards just because of his lack of a championship.

Because of the way Karl Malone delivered night in and night out for 19 seasons, he is also regarded as one of the greatest players in basketball history. Malone piled up almost 37,000 career points, are second only to Kareem. He did so by playing in top shape every single game. Even when he was nearing 40 years old, Malone could still score

20 points per game. That's how he was able to gather that amount of points in his long career.

Scoring aside, Karl Malone achieved tons in his career. He was an All-Star and an All-NBA member 14 times. He won both the regular season and All-Star MVP twice. Malone's defense wasn't shabby, either, as he was named to the All-Defensive Team four times. Though a lot of people believe it's not the best achievement, Karl Malone was a runner-up for the NBA title three times. Because of that, The Mailman has long been considered atop the list of NBA greats. *ESPN* ranks him as the 16th best player in NBA history as well as the second-best power forward.[iv] *Sports Illustrated* ranks Malone as the 17th best NBA player ever.[v] Though 16 and 17 may not seem much, it already means a lot considering that the NBA has seen hundreds of great players in a long history that has spanned since 1946.

While Father Time has long been undefeated in the history of professional sports, if there was an NBA player that had a legitimate chance of beating him, it was Karl Malone, who played at the best level possible for 19 years. There is an old saying, "Hard work beats talent when talent does not work hard." That is what Karl Malone proved, that is what The Mailman delivered.

# Final Word/About the Author

I was born and raised in Norwalk, Connecticut. Growing up, I could often be found spending many nights watching basketball, soccer, and football matches with my father in the family living room. I love sports and everything that sports can embody. I believe that sports are one of most genuine forms of competition, heart, and determination. I write my works to learn more about influential athletes in the hopes that from my writing, you the reader can walk away inspired to put in an equal if not greater amount of hard work and perseverance to pursue your goals. If you enjoyed *Karl Malone: The Remarkable Story of One of Basketball's Greatest Power Forwards*, please leave a review! Also, you can read more of my works on *Colin Kaepernick, Aaron Rodgers, Peyton Manning, Tom Brady, Russell Wilson, Michael Jordan, LeBron James, Kyrie Irving, Klay Thompson, Stephen Curry, Kevin Durant, Russell Westbrook, Anthony Davis, Chris Paul, Blake Griffin, Kobe Bryant, Joakim Noah, Scottie Pippen, Carmelo Anthony, Kevin Love, Grant Hill, Tracy McGrady, Vince Carter, Patrick Ewing, Karl Malone,*

*Tony Parker, Allen Iverson, Hakeem Olajuwon, Reggie Miller, Michael Carter-Williams, John Wall, James Harden, Tim Duncan, Steve Nash, Pau Gasol, Marc Gasol, Jimmy Butler, Dirk Nowitzki, Draymond Green, Pete Maravich, Kawhi Leonard* and *Dwyane Wade* in the Kindle Store. If you love basketball, check out my website at claytongeoffreys.com to join my exclusive list where I let you know about my latest books and give you lots of goodies.

# Like what you read? Please leave a review!

I write because I love sharing the stories of influential people like Karl Malone with fantastic readers like you. My readers inspire me to write more so please do not hesitate to let me know what you thought by leaving a review! If you love books on life, basketball, or productivity, check out my website at claytongeoffreys.com to join my exclusive list where I let you know about my latest books. Aside from being the first to hear about my latest releases, you can also download a free copy of *33 Life Lessons: Success Principles, Career Advice & Habits of Successful People*. See you there!

Clayton

# References

[i] Falk, Aaron. "How did Karl Malone fall to the Jazz in the 1985 draft?" *The Salt Lake Tribune*. 25 June 2015. Web

[ii] Falk, Aaron. "How did Karl Malone fall to the Jazz in the 1985 draft?" *The Salt Lake Tribune*. 25 June 2015. Web

[iii] Falk, Aaron. "How did Karl Malone fall to the Jazz in the 1985 draft?" *The Salt Lake Tribune*. 25 June 2015. Web

[iv] "All-Time #NBArank: Counting down the greatest players ever". *ESPN*. 3 March 2016. Web

[v] McCallum, Jack. "SI's 50 greatest players in NBA history". *Sports Illustrated*. 9 February 2016. Web

Made in the USA
Coppell, TX
11 February 2020